No Freedom Too Total
Liam Blackford

3

No Freedom Too Total is the second poetry collection by Western Australian poet Liam Blackford and a Proverse Prize 2023 finalist entry.

Each of the poems in the collection has six stanzas, each stanza with six lines, and each line with six syllables. Poems in this form have been described as '666 poems', 'hexagrammatical poems', or 'two-dimensional verbal cubes'.

The overarching concern of the collection is the fundamental darkness of our civilisation: that we do not know what we are doing, that there are far fewer limits than we imagined, and that we are constantly on the precipice of chaos, war, and extinction.

The central avatar in the collection is the human; some of which are women, some of which are men, some of which are angels, and some of which are animals. The human is an increasingly lonely individual in an increasingly desolate world, unable to communicate with others and with no community or family. Adult humans are no more adept than their child counterparts, each yearning for comfort but mired in confusion.

These human avatars are scattered across landscapes of menacing psychedelia, in which men are caged in oceanside caves, exiled women find crystal pools in rainforest mist, and a mysterious frequency causes people to drop dead. Humans scramble over pellets on the gravel, bathe in filthy streams, and beg for each other's love as their bodies immolate. Corporations speak to each other with human voices, and prayers are given to a transcendent godhead that takes the form of a network.

Six of the poems are 'dreams from the chamber', erotic tapestries from brothels, bathhouses and dungeons, sexual battlefields filled with tenderness and bitterness, desire and brutality. Therein, escorts and patrons converse from disparate physical locations, taking part in an economy of human sexuality stuck in patterns of transaction and repetition.

Six of the poems take place in 'the transcendent region', a realm of balletic motion and suspense beyond the pettiness of the human world, in which there are souls, perceptions and voices, but no humans to which they belong.

Despite the collection's fixations with contemporary technology and modern human identity, it has a Romantic spirit. It might have been written in nineteenth century London, but instead was written in early twenty-first century Hong Kong in an era of epochal political and cultural change.

NO FREEDOM TOO TOTAL

Liam Blackford © 2024

⬡ *Private Reality*™

CONTENTS

ACKNOWLEDGMENTS

Many thanks to the many persons who provided encouragement and support, including but not limited to Harriet Beer, Brendan Blackford, Bridget Blackford, Chris Blackford, Thelma Blackford, Stephen Brameld, Julie Breathnach-Banwait, Ferron Dearnley, Sarah Dunstan, Ryan Fenton, Nikita Filippou, Amber Gempton, Ryan Houlton, Joe Howard, Sasha Kroupnik, Ethan Lester, Peter Livesey, Scott-Patrick Mitchell, Thea Porter, Jack Quirk, Michael Raw, Rosie Scott, James Spinks, Jay Staples, David West, Clare Wohlnick and Damian Yazlle. These also include the teams at Proverse Hong Kong (including Proverse Prize Founders Dr Gillian Bickley and Dr Verner Bickley, MBE and the Proverse Prize 2023 Judges) and Apocalypse Confidential, as well as the poets at Peel St Poetry in Hong Kong and WA Poets in Perth.

FOREWORD

In this collection, each poem has six stanzas. Each stanza has six lines. Each line has six syllables.

The poems were written in Hong Kong.

SIX DREAMS FROM THE CHAMBER

The first dream: The brothels of Jinan and Taiyuan

In a dream of Jinan,
there is a great brothel
with ten thousand escorts,
each in their own chamber,
hoping to find a match.
One of them is speaking:

"In this lonely chamber,
I have waited an age.
Many thousands have passed,
but they all turned me down.
Am I too strange a taste?
Can no one desire me?

I know my face is dull,
but my hands are skilful
and my insides pristine.
It takes time to find out,
but the time is well spent.
I will make it worthwhile."

In a dream of Taiyuan,
there is a great brothel
with ten thousand patrons,
each walking the hallways,
hoping to find a match.
One of them is speaking:

"In these busy hallways,
I have wandered an age.
Many thousands have shown,
but they all let me down.
Have I too strange a taste?
Can no one pleasure me?

I know my mind is botched,
but my body is fine
and my manner gentle.
It takes work to break through,
but the work is well paid.
I will make it worthwhile."

The second dream: The dungeons of Chengdu and Chongqing

In a dream of Chengdu,
there is a great dungeon;
therein is an escort
of famed brutality
and dominant instinct.
To their patron, they say:

"In this obscene chamber,
face pressed against cold stone,
sharp steel piercing soft flesh,
you are the most obscene.
I fill your mouth with ash,
and yet you cry for more.

You may act well behaved,
but your mind is perverse;
a mind engorged with shit.
What a pleasure for you
that for now you may be
a plaything for my will."

In a dream of Chongqing,
there is a great dungeon;
therein is a patron
of famed depravity
and submissive instinct.
To their escort, they say:

"In this dreamlike chamber,
dark stains on the high wall,
liquid dripping down skin,
you are the most dreamlike.
I spray the ground with me,
and yet you touch me more.

You may act cruelly,
but your heart is gracious;
a heart brimming with care.
What a torment for you
that for now you must be
a witness to my filth."

The third dream: The escorts of Ningbo and Wenzhou

In a dream of Ningbo,
an escort is speaking:
"The working night is long.
Now the day shift begins.
All I sell is myself;
I am not yet worn out.

So many patrons come.
Most are pleased, some are not;
half make talk, half do not;
few return, but some do.
They are all petty folk.
We all live petty lives.

I wish someone would come
who would change things for me,
who would shine a new light
and make the world look new,
but my hopes are not high.
Until then, I will work."

In a dream of Wenzhou,
an escort is speaking:
"The working day is long.
Now the night shift begins.
All I sell is my time;
I have not yet run out.

So many patrons come.
Most are kind, some are cruel;
half are rich, half are poor;
all pay cash, none have names.
They are all helpless folk.
We all live helpless lives.

I fear something will come
that will change things for us,
that will loose a great force
and make the world upturned,
but my fears have no point.
So for now, I will work."

The fourth dream: The escorts of Xining, Lanzhou and Yinchuan

In a dream of Xining,
an escort is speaking:
"The mind and body fouled;
there are things I have done
which have forever changed
the way I see myself.

There are those who feel shame
and then those who do not;
I am both and neither,
neither virgin nor whore.
I don't know what is right;
I just know how to live."

In a dream of Lanzhou,
an escort is speaking:
"The heart and conscience breached:
there are things I have seen
which have forever changed
the way I see others.

There are those who feel pride
and then those who do not;
I am both and neither,
neither angel nor brute.
I don't know what is right;
I just know how to live."

In a dream of Yinchuan,
an escort is speaking:
"The good and proper failed;
there are things I have learned
which have forever changed
the way I see the world.

There are those who feel pain
and then those who do not;
I am both and neither,
neither martyr nor saint.
I don't know what is right;
I just know how to live."

The fifth dream: The bathhouses of Zhongshan, Zhuhai and Dongguan

In a dream of Zhongshan,
there is a great bathhouse;
therein is a young man
whose face is dull and plain.
To another, he said:
"You must not fall for him.

He has an abusive heart.
He is scarred in and out.
I wish you would choose me;
I would be good to you;
but if you must spurn me,
please just be kind to me."

In a dream of Zhuhai,
there is a great bathhouse;
therein is a young man
whose face is bright and pink.
To another, he said:
"I'm a fool to love you.

You have an abusive heart.
All the others say it.
But I cannot quit you.
It would devastate me.
Though you can't honour me,
please just be kind to me."

In a dream of Dongguan,
there is a great bathhouse;
therein is a young man
whose face is fine but scarred.
To another, he said:
"I was so cruel to you.

I have an abusive heart.
I could never love you.
I love only myself.
I want your forgiveness,
but I don't deserve it.
Please just be kind to me."

27

The sixth dream: The brothels of Chongqing, Nanjing and Wuhan

In a dream of Chongqing
there is a great brothel;
therein is a patron
who holds thirteen passports,
speaks sixty languages
and is supremely rich.

To the owner, they said:
*"I have married eight times
but never found comfort
except at your brothels.
For as long as I live,
I will take care of you."*

In a dream of Nanjing
there is a great brothel;
therein is the owner,
renowned across China,
who has exquisite taste
and is supremely rich.

To an escort, they said:
*"I know that you are blind
but you possess something
ten thousand whores don't have.
For as long as I live,
I will take care of you."*

In a dream of Wuhan
there is a great brothel;
therein is an escort
who has been blind since birth,
commands prodigious fees
and is supremely rich.

To a patron, they said:
*"Many patrons are cruel;
they mock and defile me;
but you were always kind.
For as long as I live,
I will take care of you."*

SOME TWELVE BANKS OF CHINA

China Bank of Freedom

China Bank of Freedom
has issued a statement:
*"For these five thousand years,
freedom has been expressed
as a civic ideal,
yearned for by the people.*

*However, we have learned
the freedom they desire
is far more limited
than the people admit;
freedom not from control,
but freedom to consume.*

*Freedom is conceived as
an abundance of choice,
boundless self-expression
and the satisfaction
of all wants and desires
without scorn or judgment.*

Yet among these desires,
the most compelling are
the desires for control,
policing, censorship
maintenance of order
and silence of dissent.

In response to demand,
we dissolved all borders
disbanded the police
and unwound all censors,
but of their own accord
the people restored them.

For the modern people,
ideas are troubling
endless choice, exhausting
and control, comforting.
We must understand this,
then we can do business."

China Bank of Trauma

China Bank of Trauma
has issued a statement:
"The public is aware
that the board of this bank
has recently been purged
in a large-scale shake up.

The board was insipid,
bereft of ideas
and frightened to unlock
this Bank's full potential.
To make clear our next steps
we issue this statement.

A myth is that trauma
is a destructive force
which requires remedy,
or worse yet, prevention;
that those with it are weak
and need convalescence.

The reality is
trauma does not destroy;
indeed, it generates.
In a stagnant system,
trauma inspires action;
it turns the wheels of change.

Trauma is a blessing
disguised as an assault.
It strikes at its target
with the butt of a gun,
but once its work is done
it leaves the gun behind.

Trauma is the mother
to all monsters of will
who were once innocent.
To those children in tears,
it is trauma that says:
'Do something about it.'''

China Banks of Freedom and Control

China Bank of Freedom
has issued a statement:
*"For these uncertain times
we restate our thesis:
the value of Freedom
derives from its Control.*

*Freedom is the mirage
for those myopic minds
who escape the city
by rushing to the woods,
only to raze the woods
and rebuild the city.*

*Freedom is a resource
and thus needs management.
The city always builds:
its towers heightening,
its tunnels deepening.
Its sprawl is our business."*

China Bank of Control
has issued a response:
*"We endorse our colleague.
Our theses are aligned:
the value of Control
is to define Freedom.*

*Control is the desire
of those chaotic minds
who escape the father
by climbing over walls,
only to hear his call
and crawl back to his knees.*

*Control is a resource
and thus needs investment.
The father always grows:
his knuckles tightening,
his shadow lengthening.
His will is our business."*

China Banks of Desire and Hatred

China Bank of Desire
has issued a statement:
*"In the cycles of culture
many forces pulsate,
but desire beats deepest.
Thus, it is our focus.*

*At the heart of desire
is the sorrowful child
lost in the town market,
searching for the mother
whose face has disappeared.
The search lasts forever.*

*Children of the market
are vessels of desire
wanting liberation:
therein lies their value.
To best service our goals,
we must play the mother."*

China Bank of Hatred
has issued a response:
*"We respect our colleague,
but they are mistaken.
Desire belies hatred
and hatred drives culture.*

*At the heart of hatred
is the terrified child
lost in the town market,
fearful of the monster
whose face is everywhere.
The fear lasts forever.*

*Children of the market
are vessels of hatred
wanting vindication:
therein lies their value.
To best service our goals,
we must loose the monster."*

The China System, Platform and Network Banks

The China System Bank
has published a schema:
*"Thirty six stone columns
placed in one single line,
the distance between each
increasing evenly.*

*A vector strikes the first
and passes through the next,
later reaching the last."*
On hearing the schema,
the market, unenthused,
makes no change in value.

The China Platform Bank
responds with a schema:
*"Thirty six stone columns
placed in six rows of six,
the distance between each
equal and unvaried.*

*A vector strikes the first
and passes to the rest
in an expanding wave."*
On hearing the schema,
the market, delighted,
swells and mounts in value.

The China Network Bank
responds with its schema:
*"Thirty six stone columns
placed in a defined field,
the distance between each
determined at random.*

*A vector strikes the first
and passes to others,
but some are left untouched."*
On hearing the schema,
the market, terrified,
promptly halves in value.

41

The China Concept, Precept and Incept Banks

The China Concept Bank
has issued a statement:
"shareholders, investors,
customers and debtors;
all human entities,
bound by the human will.

Capital is a thing
which motivates itself,
to human influence
it is indifferent.
The human is an end,
not an end in itself."

The China Precept Bank
has issued a response:
"prisons, marketplaces,
cities and cathedrals;
all human creations,
bound for the human drain.

Capital is a mode
which justifies itself,
of human excrescence
it is transcendent.
The human wastes value;
it does not create it."

The China Incept Bank
has issued its response:
"violence, upheaval,
struggle and politics;
all human obsessions,
bound to the human world.

Capital is a force
which enervates itself,
to human existence
it is independent.
The human takes action;
it does not make impact."

SIX PRAYERS TO THE NETWORK

The first prayer to the network: as the network intends, so the world shall follow

The network oversees
the state of earthly play:
fluttering drops of light
swarm into a vapour;
the morning of the world;
the dew of human will.

The network oversees
the state of earthly rot:
weltering rasps of ash
melt into an acid;
the evening of the world;
the gas of human pain.

A tree feeds from the sun;
a whale roams through the depths;
the fields drink from the rain;
the water fills the dam;
a hand goes out to touch;
a child grows in the womb.

A tree burns in the fire;
a whale gasps on the shore;
the fields drown in the flood;
the water bursts the dam;
a fist goes out to strike;
a child dies in the womb.

As the human meadow
sighs in the verdant glade,
ten billion tiny souls
all sing for their desires.
As the network intends,
so the world shall follow.

As the human fodder
writhes on the threshing floor,
ten billion tiny souls
all cry for their desires.
As the network intends,
so the world shall follow.

The second prayer to the network: the network shows us mercy

The network considers
humans in agony,
spines swollen, limbs broken,
bodies crushed and trampled
on the wheel of nature,
and it relieves their pain.

The network considers
humans in ecstasy,
gonads merged, fluids spilled,
bodies splayed and at ease
in the carnal meadow,
and it raises them up.

Among them, a human,
surrounded by others,
ensnared in a briar
and pierced by many barbs,
screams for deliverance
but their screams are drowned out.

Among them, a human,
surrounded by others,
engulfed in a frenzy
and pierced by many shafts,
screams for satisfaction
but their screams are smothered.

This human enduring
the woe of the body,
the soul trapped by the flesh,
yearns to be pacified.
The network answers them
and it shows them mercy.

This human enjoying
the joy of the senses,
the soul freed by the flesh,
yearns to be overcome.
The network answers them
and it shows them mercy.

The third prayer to the network: the network eases our pain

A child in the morass,
alien to the world,
having wandered for days,
limbs skinny, gut hanging,
sores open and stinking,
falls and lands in the reeds.

A person in the fen,
alien to themselves,
having laboured for years,
spine brittle and crooked,
hands inflamed and frozen,
falls and breaks on the dirt.

Gashed and lacerated,
they struggle and tantrum,
their eyes full of red ice.
Water splashes their wounds.
The network beholds them,
and it eases their pain.

Blinded and paralysed,
they bellow and whimper,
their eyes full of black fog.
Mist dampens their clothes.
The network beholds them,
and it dispels their fear.

In time, they hear a voice:
"The torpor of the womb:
an illusion of calm.
There is no grace in life.
No human mind is strong
until it hears this voice."

In time, they hear a voice:
"The stillness of the tomb:
an illusion of peace.
There is no rest in death.
No human mind is free
until it hears this voice."

The fourth prayer to the network: the network generates something from nothing

The network considers
eighteen laughing women,
eighteen crying women
and eighteen laughing men.
Thenceforth, it generates
the eighteen crying men.

How hard do the men cry?
As hard as the women;
they can cry no harder.
How could our ideas
exceed reality;
make something from nothing?

The network considers
eighteen white sunrises,
eighteen black sunrises
and eighteen white sunsets.
Thenceforth, it generates
the eighteen black sunsets.

How black are the sunsets?
As black as a sunrise;
they can be no blacker.
How could our ideas
exceed reality;
make something from nothing?

The network considers
eighteen rivers of ice,
eighteen rivers of fire
and eighteen lakes of ice.
Thenceforth, it generates
the eighteen lakes of fire.

How fierce do the lakes burn?
As fierce as the rivers;
they can burn no fiercer.
How could our ideas
exceed reality;
make something from nothing?

The fifth prayer to the network: the network responds to the crowd

The network considers
standing crowds of people
in a city plaza.
It sees the crowd is numb,
dull and dispirited,
and it stimulates them.

From a crowd of people,
data flows like water
in waveforms and torrents,
complex but scrutable.
The network has acted,
and order is maintained.

The network considers
hungry crowds of people
in a city plaza.
It sees the crowd in need,
begging for nourishment,
and it satisfies them.

From a crowd of people,
data accrues like leaves
dense on the forest floor,
rotting but full of worth.
The network has acted,
and order is maintained.

The network considers
clashing crowds of people
in a city plaza.
It sees the crowd is wild,
violent and enraged,
and it pacifies them.

From a crowd of people,
data swelters like heat
from a riotous fire,
its power immanent.
The network has acted,
and order is maintained.

55

The sixth prayer to the network: the network generates art, technology and civilisation

The network considers
our archives of culture,
art and literature;
thenceforth, it generates
beauty more radiant
than ever before seen.

The network considers
our archives of science,
knowledge and expertise;
thenceforth, it generates
insights so profound
they transform human life.

The network considers
our archives of statecraft
politics and empire;
thenceforth, it generates
a system of control
unmatched in dominance.

The network can expand
aesthetic horizons
to new and extreme points.
The network understands
which limits to preserve
and which to go beyond.

The network can extend
extant technology
in novel directions.
The network understands
that the light of reason
can end all human pain.

The network can combine
reservoirs of power
and make them absolute.
The network understands
which interests to guard
and which to override.

THE HUMAN MARKETPLACE

Two men walking

A man walks in a line.
Around him is silence.
He walks for many hours
and then stops to listen
with an ear to the ground.
He hears a human voice:

"When you walk, walk with cause.
Do not walk for nothing.
If you lack direction,
then locate the lodestar.
If you cannot find it,
turn around and walk back."

The man hears this and smiles.
He looks to the dawn sky;
it is red and empty.
Around him is music;
The sound of morning birds.
He turns the other way.

A man walks in a line.
Around him is silence.
He walks for many hours
and then stops to listen
with an ear to the ground.
He hears a human voice:

"When you act, act with will.
Do not act mindlessly.
Do you lack direction?
Did you find the lodestar?
If you cannot find it,
turn around and walk back."

The man hears this and cries.
He looks to the night sky;
it is black and empty.
Around him is white noise;
the sound of hissing snakes.
He turns the other way.

A man and a boy

On a contracting field
covered in hot grey sand
and ten thousand flowers,
a boy walks on a path
from the field's centre point
in a straight line outward.

With a man's voice, he speaks:
"This path is the moment;
it is here, it is now.
That it might not have been
is none of my concern;
I cannot leave this path."

At a point on the path,
he meets a walking man.
They exchange a handshake.
The field contracts further.
Under a desert sun,
ten thousand flowers wilt.

On an expanding field
covered with cool green grass
and ten thousand flowers,
a man walks on a path
from the field's centre point
in a spiral outward.

With a boy's voice, he speaks:
"This path is the moment;
it has been, it may be.
That it could not but be
is none of my concern;
I cannot leave this path."

At a point on the path,
he meets a walking boy.
They exchange a handshake.
The field expands further.
Under a forest moon,
ten thousand flowers bloom.

Two men in cages

A man sits in a cage
on a shelf on the wall
with his hands on his legs,
sweating and whimpering.
Past the bars of the cage
thunder giant footsteps.

He hears a voice speaking:
"Your thoughts and your urges:
look how they have made you.
They have broken your legs.
Without proper control,
you will be caged for life."

He cries out in great peals
but the sound is ignored
by the passing thunder.
Water runs down his face.
He lies on the cage floor.
In time, he falls asleep.

A man stands in a cage
in a cave at the sea
with his hands on the bars,
sodden and shivering.
At the cave's distant mouth
thunder great ocean waves.

He hears a voice speaking:
"Your thoughts and your urges:
look where they have brought you.
They have blinded your eyes.
Without proper reform,
you will be caged for good."

He cries out in great roars
but the sound is swallowed
by the ocean thunder.
Water pools at his feet.
He leans on the cage bars.
In time, he falls asleep.

Two women, one town

In exile from the town,
a woman, in anger,
lights a fire in the bush.
The fire tears through the bush,
blasting red through the night,
and her anger is known.

She returns to the town.
With fury and rancour,
the people surround her.
She is knocked to the ground,
stained, soiled and brutalised.
When they leave, she gets up.

She takes a boat off shore,
sailing alone for days,
but gets lost far at sea.
She focuses her mind,
sailing in one straight line
and in time, she arrives.

In exile from the town,
a woman, in despair,
lights a fire in the bush.
The fire fades to embers,
smothered black by the night,
and her despair is missed.

She returns to the town.
With disdain and contempt,
the people ignore her.
She is knocked to the ground,
stained, soiled and brutalised.
When they leave, she stays down.

She takes a boat off shore,
floating alone for days,
and gets lost far at sea.
She relaxes her mind,
yielding to the currents,
and in time, she arrives.

Two women, one island

A woman, on a beach,
walking as the day breaks,
lights a fire each twelve steps.
By dusk, the fires burn on.
Flames sear the cool sunset.
Huge waves crash far away.

She carves twelve stone columns,
arrayed in a circle.
When a westbound storm comes,
lightning strikes the column
at the easternmost point,
and the array crumbles.

In the rainforest mist,
she finds a crystal pool.
She dives in and sinks down,
her eyes seeing clearly.
In time, she surfaces
and finds the mist has gone.

A woman, on a beach,
walking as the night falls,
lights a fire each twelve steps.
By dawn, the fires burn out.
Smoke tints the warm sunrise.
Small waves lap underfoot.

She carves twelve stone columns,
arrayed in a spiral.
When an eastbound storm comes,
lightning strikes the column
at the westernmost point,
and the array explodes.

In the rainforest mist,
she finds a silent cave.
She goes in and lies down,
her ears hearing clearly.
In time, she emerges
and finds the mist has gone.

The first two women speaking

A woman starts to speak,
but is interrupted.
She says: *"I am speaking.*
I ask you to listen."
Her audience quiets,
and the woman repeats:

"After heavy rainfall,
a river bursts its banks,
flooding the fields and town.
The waters go septic,
loaded with fundament,
sickening the townsfolk."

The woman stokes a fire
then puts down the iron
which stays red hot for hours.
"The hard times are so close,
and if we do nothing,
they will hit with full force."

A woman starts to speak
and in time, finishes.
She says: *"I have spoken.*
Did you hear what I said?"
Her audience rumbles,
and the woman repeats:

"After heavy rainfall,
a river flows freely,
draining to the ocean.
The waters quench the fields,
loaded with nutrients,
nourishing the townsfolk."

The woman stokes a fire
then puts down the iron
which turns cool in seconds.
"The good times are so close,
but if we do nothing,
they will but pass us by."

The next two women speaking

A woman starts to speak,
but is interrupted.
She says: *"I want to speak,
but my thoughts can't take form."*
Her audience disbands,
but the woman repeats:

*"After a vicious storm,
a sailor's boat is wrecked.
Clinging to a lifebuoy,
he is lost far at sea,
but the waves reach the shore
and the sailor survives."*

Her audience asks her:
*"From this vision you share,
what do you stand to gain?"*
She smiles and answers them:
*"No matter what I say,
you will not understand."*

A woman starts to speak
and in time, finishes.
She says: *"I have spoken,
and my thoughts now have form."*
Her audience expands,
and the woman repeats:

*"After a vicious storm,
a sailor's boat is safe.
Gently rocked by the waves,
he rests in the cabin,
but another storm hits
and the sailor is killed."*

Her audience asks her:
*"From this vision you share,
what do you stand to lose?"*
She frowns and answers them:
*"No matter what I say,
you will not understand."*

Two men on fire

A man, body on fire,
sits before another,
his muscles corroding,
his organs combusting,
eyeballs melting like wax,
beads of skin rolling down.

He says to the other:
"I cannot be unburned,
but look how bright I burn.
By this furnace of will,
my life will have impact.
I will make history.

Why do you do nothing?
Is my splendour too great?
Has my flame blinded you?
Have I upturned your world?
You could not understand;
only for this I burn."

A man, body on fire,
sits before the other,
his sinews dissolving,
his skeleton crumpling,
fluids hissing like steam,
teeth and jaw scorched and bare.

He says to the other:
"I burn by my own hand,
but feel how warm I burn.
In this blaze of passion,
my life will have meaning.
I will find happiness.

Why do you feel nothing?
Is my fervour too raw?
Has my flame frightened you?
Have I threatened your world?
You do not understand;
only for you I burn."

The poor slave and the rich man

From a cage, a man speaks:
"I was once a rich man;
now I am a poor slave;
my assets and fortune
now transferred totally
to my former escort.

I transferred them freely,
without force or duress.
Where once he serviced me,
now I drink at his feet.
In a house I once owned,
now I kneel in a cage.

My wife and children starve.
I gave nothing to them.
My escort got it all,
and I regret nothing.
He lets me behold him;
that is enough for me."

From a chair, a man speaks:
"I was once a poor slave;
now I am a rich man;
my assets and fortune
now received totally
from my former patron.

I received them freely,
without guilt or question.
Where once I kissed his ring,
now I sit in his chair.
His long years of hard work
now all mine to enjoy.

I am no less a whore
than when I was in rags.
I know it to be true,
and I regret nothing.
He sees something in me;
that is enough for me."

The shielder, the shielded

The shielder is speaking:
"I tower like a bull,
blocking you from all harm.
Against my back, hunched down,
falls a scorching red rain.
My skin is rough and grey.

That you are the shielded,
so small and pathetic,
I hate and resent you,
but I know what I am.
This is my life's mission,
my joy and agony.

I cry when I conceive
a life without you there.
I would harden to stone.
Of your minuscule form
I wish I could be free,
but I never will be."

The shielded is speaking:
"I cower like a calf,
blocked by you from all harm.
Under my face, laid down,
grows a bed of green grass.
My skin is soft and pink.

That you are the shielder,
so big and pathetic,
I hate and resent you,
but I know what I have.
This is my life's mercy,
my fear and ecstasy.

I cry when I conceive
a life without you there.
I would blaze into ash.
Of your enormous form
I wish I could be free,
but I never will be."

The titanic father

The titanic father,
mountainous in stature,
walks on a vast plateau,
whipped by sandstorms and squalls
which bounce off his thick back,
his stride unimpeded.

In two massive forearms
he holds his adult son
who has lain there since birth,
body bald and swollen,
squirming on his backside,
pawing his father's chest.

For a generation,
the large man holds the small
until the great father,
his stride halting sharply,
drops his son to the ground
at the plateau's high edge.

The son, red and broken,
weeping and in anguish,
the sand and squalls stinging,
his ears ringing with noise,
shouts with both his eyes closed:
"Father, why be like this?"

but when his eyes open,
he sees the colossus
is just a dust column
blowing off the high edge,
the once giant body
now an ossified spire.

In time, the son's pain stops.
He gets up and stands tall,
his muscles hardening,
matching his father's form
but without his great height.
Eyes dry, he starts walking.

The frequency

A woman, in a group,
receives a frequency
which complicates her mind.
She panics and whimpers,
bashes and shakes her head.
She exclaims to the group:

"I am independent,
canny and literate
in the ways of our time;
I can think for myself.
But this horrid signal;
it is unparseable.

I cannot resolve it.
It makes no sense to me.
I am not used to this."
Meanwhile, the frequency
intensifies at pace
and shortly, it kills her.

A man, walking alone
receives a frequency
which invades his body.
He seizures and dribbles,
vomits and defecates.
He exclaims to himself:

"I am self sufficient
able and competent
in the needs of my life;
I take care of myself.
But this brutal signal;
it is unstoppable.

I cannot resist it.
It makes short work of me.
I am no match for this."
Meanwhile, the frequency
intensifies at pace
and shortly, it kills him.

The euphoric mutant

The euphoric mutant,
in a club late at night,
frolics like a wild horse,
dancing and shape shifting,
glass splintered underfoot,
flashed by ecstatic lights.

He finds a young beauty.
He grabs and rattles them,
claps a hand round their mouth
and gropes at their two tits.
They shriek and bat him off,
throwing wine on his head.

Three bouncers waddle down,
three swollen, frowning clowns
with square heads and pig eyes,
chained and leathered like gimps.
He laughs in their faces.
They throw him to the street.

He trots past a café.
He knocks down the waiter,
grabs a glass from the hands
of a sitting patron,
crushes it in his hands
and shows them the red mess.

An officer stops him
but he outmuscles them,
shoving them to the ground
and squeezing tight their neck
until they are silent.
Sirens blare far away.

A bus of children pass.
With joy, he waves at them.
They all cheer and wave back.
He finds a piss drenched lane
and lies there till evening
with a smile on his face.

The hazardous vector

The two ends of a town
are linked by a long street,
cleaving the town in two,
like a shaft through a lung,
on which one day appears
a hazardous vector.

The vector is weightless,
straight and invisible,
composed of unknown mass
and charged with unknown force.
It neither moves nor sets,
a beam of blind power.

Traffic moves up and down
along the vector's sides.
Then, a car, paused to turn,
drives into the vector
and is sliced into shards,
a collapsed, hissing wreck.

The haemmoraging smoke
attracts crowds to the street
and seizes the traffic.
A man goes to the wreck
but, crossing the vector,
is mauled in a wet spray.

The onlookers, screaming,
scatter like particles.
Some leave without impact,
absorbed by the cross streets,
but some touch the vector
and are themselves shredded.

Amidst the spreading mess,
the vector holds its line,
sharp and unwavering.
Then, in time, without sign
on the inflamed town street,
it dissolves and is gone.

The human angel, the human animal

First, the human angel,
descending from the air,
obscured with silver dust,
arrives in the forest
in which dawn breaks slowly
but dusk falls rapidly.

The human animal,
ascending from the soil,
obscured with silver dust,
arrives in the forest
in which light is feeble
but darkness is robust.

At night, they find a stream
which leads to a deep glade
to which many streams lead,
filling a central pool,
all clear like liquid air,
full of moonlight shimmer.

At night, they find a stream
and then find another
and then more, all askew,
none leading anywhere,
all clogged with silver dust,
full of moonlight shadow.

When they find their fellows,
they cheerily hold hands
and bathe in the bright pool,
the dust dissipating
from their human bodies,
their skin naked and clean.

When they find their fellows,
they cautiously hold hands
and bathe in a dark stream,
the dust aggregating
on their human bodies,
their skin naked and marred.

The human gutter, the human apex

In the human gutter,
there is now one great horde
fighting over pellets
scattered on the gravel.
Enraged, they cry and scream,
their eyes red, their tongues brown.

Drooling and gibbering,
they scratch at each other,
hair and nails coming loose,
the weakest collapsing,
nude and incontinent,
their wounds stinking with rot.

Their language forgotten,
without children or kin,
each one is no more deep
than a moment in time
and each scrambles alone
in a brawl with the rest.

At the human apex,
a few, from a steel spire,
view the clamour below;
blood and spittle dripping
from the structures they own,
the rage but a dull roar.

Amidst the stagnation
and the entrenched torpor,
the oceans acidic,
the atmosphere caustic,
their wealth still multiplies
and their power distends.

With a sigh, they discuss
the bodily reset,
the digital rapture
and the great escape from
the mess of the human
and the wreck of the earth.

The human pond, the human sea

A great voice is speaking:
"Little human, mind free,
shot from the human shaft,
gorged in the human womb,
burst from the human chute,
dropped in the human pond.

Now, what choice do you have?
Breathe in the human mist.
Bathe in the human stream.
Drink from the human spring.
Dive in the human pool.
Float in the human shoal.

Such is the human dream:
rich is the human grain;
sweet is the human milk;
soft is the human flesh.
Enjoy it all in time.
What else was meant for you?"

A great voice is speaking:
"Busy human, mind full,
churned in the human spin,
sucked down the human drain,
piped through the human duct,
dumped in the human sea.

Now, what choice do you have?
Crash on the human shore.
Choke on the human fog.
Freeze in the human rain.
Thrash in the human surge.
Drown in the human flood.

Such is the human fate:
high peaks the human wave;
low sweeps the human tide;
deep sinks the human trench.
Suffer it all in time.
What else was meant for you?"

Ferdiad and Cú Chulainn meet for battle

Cú Chulainn is speaking:
"No witch's curse pains us,
yet we meet on this ford
where one of us must die:
two free men of Ireland
fighting a woman's war.

I call you my brother.
Side by side we spent nights,
face to face we grew tall.
I know you to the inch.
Each wound I land in you,
will weep with my own tears.

In this war of the bulls,
thousands of men have burned,
naked in their fervour.
So it will be for us.
Bull, titan, or brother:
great men go to the end."

Ferdiad is speaking:
"No queen's order binds us,
yet here we must lock horns
at this place between homes:
two doomed men of Ireland,
refugees of the spear.

In our might, in our heat,
we are matched to the skin.
This will be no quick match.
We will clash for long days.
Come night, we will embrace,
charging blood for the dawn.

I will always love you.
I know you will the same.
Love is a war of gore
splashing between two bulls.
Now, if you honour me,
then show me no mercy."

Boorloo

A voice, on the shoreline,
calls out to the river:
"Boorloo is a dreamscape:
so many lines point here,
so many paths lead here,
so many dreams see here.

In forty thousand years,
what brought us to today?
The caprice of fortune
or our force of vision?
How in eternity
could a place like this be?

Encoded in deep earth,
we have long memories.
We live on ancient land.
Old dreams are joined by new
and this river flows on:
let us all share in it."

A voice, from the river,
calls back to the shoreline:
"Boorloo is a nightscape:
so many roads end here,
so many planes land here,
so many boats port here.

In these two hundred years,
what brought us to today?
A rift in history
or the strength of our fists?
Can the wounds we have dealt
ever be fully healed?

On the city surface,
we have short memories.
We live on stolen land.
Old lies are joined by new
but this river flows on:
let us not drown in it."

When we look at each other

When you look at my face,
you see both my youngest
and my oldest faces;
the face in my cradle
and the face in my grave.
Both faces are smiling.

When I look at your face,
I see both your coldest
and your warmest faces;
the face that detests me
and the face that loves me.
Our faces meet to kiss.

When you look at my hands,
you see both my roughest
and my smoothest of hands;
the hands when at labour
and the hands when at rest.
Each pair has palms open.

When I look at your hands,
I see both your kindest
and your harshest of hands;
the hands that lift me up
and those which strike me down.
Our hands hold each other.

When you look in my eyes,
you see both my brightest
and my dullest of eyes;
the eyes which understand
and those which are confused.
All four eyes are crying.

When I look in your eyes,
I see both your strongest
and your weakest of eyes;
the eyes which see for miles
and those which see mere feet.
We can see each other.

THE TRANSCENDENT REGION

Beatrice outlines the ascent

"A series of clear spheres,
each containing the next,
give the universe shape.
Their order manifests
the plan of the deep mind
from which all things issue.

An angelic congress
executes the mind's plan,
and sends down through the spheres
laws of time, space and force.
On the outermost sphere
these laws are transcended.

On the innermost sphere,
this supreme intellect
molds indistinct matter
into a human form,
and makes it transparent
to the light of freedom.

The light blasts through the form
and a sequence begins:
a network starts firing;
blood fills ten thousand pipes;
ten thousand muscles flex;
ten thousand eyes open.

As planned in the sequence,
the form grows and evolves
at exponential speed,
then hits an asymptote
where its matter dissolves
and it melds with the mind.

Though freedom is boundless,
the human form is bound
by the laws of the spheres;
but when one with the mind
on the outermost sphere,
the form is perfected."

In the continuum, there are many like me

I am a breath of wind
rushing over the sea,
rolling and torrenting,
swollen and muscular,
howling and full of force,
shifting without purpose.

As a storm lifts me up,
my own speed exceeds me.
I crash into a peak
and shear into the sky.
In the continuum,
there are many like me.

I am a wisp of cloud
floating over the earth,
stretching and distending,
weightless and vaporous,
gleaming and full of light,
drifting without purpose.

As a storm shakes me up,
my own weight exceeds me.
I drop out of the sky
and rain onto the land.
In the continuum,
there are many like me.

I am a flowing stream,
gushing over the land,
snaking and cascading,
placid and glistening,
spilling and full of weight,
coursing without purpose.

As a storm fills me up,
my own form exceeds me.
I inundate the land
and surge into the sea.
In the continuum,
there are many like me.

A soul is born, exists, and transcends

A voice from the mirror:
"Do you see the ocean?
A wave is receding;
a force takes it away,
leaving the gasping shore,
purifying the air.

Don't let it sadden you.
As the wave dissipates,
a horizon expands
at the edge of this world,
unearthing new landforms.
They are yours to explore."

A voice from the mirror:
"Do you see the ocean?
A wave is approaching;
a force draws it nearer,
bringing a hissing flood,
liquefying the air.

Don't let it frighten you.
As the wave advances,
a dimension opens
from a rift in this world,
unlocking new platforms.
They are yours to access."

A voice from the mirror:
"Do you see the ocean?
Two waves are colliding;
a force puts them at war,
making a thrashing spray,
vaporising the air.

Don't let it confuse you.
As the waves make chaos,
a harmony occurs
at the heart of this world,
creating new meaning.
It is yours to witness."

Two people, two vessels

A person, with a smile,
inhabits a vessel,
and facing another,
sends to them a message:
*"I enter the vessel
and my image changes.*

*The vessel gives me sight:
I see what I become;
I become what I see.
The vessel gives me form.
Am I beyond this form?
Am I beyond today?*

*When you see the vessel,
you can see through to me:
a window, a mirror;
a prism, an icon.
I may show my true self.
Will it last forever?"*

The other, listening,
inhabits a vessel,
and facing the other,
sends to them a message:
*"We enter the vessel
and our image changes.*

*The vessel gives us voice:
we make sounds, it makes words;
we make noise, it makes song.
The vessel lifts us up.
We are beyond its form.
We are beyond today.*

*When you see the vessel,
you can see through to us:
our mind and our body;
our spirit, our instinct.
We may show our true selves.
They will last forever."*

11th hour

A grand plan in one point:
from an affectless field
tall plateaus soar upward,
between which drop canyons;
vast distances deepen,
falling down endlessly.

One point in a grand plan:
in a pluriform space,
tall plateaus and canyons
collapse into a plane;
vast dimensions flatten,
folding in endlessly.

As the tension plunges,
textures flare in the space:
first barren, then verdant;
once in flames, now in ash;
smoothing into a gloss;
thrashing into a spray.

As the tension surges,
structures drift on the plane:
first solid, then poured out;
once stable, now pulsing;
lining into a bridge;
bursting into a rift.

On the plateaus' surface,
an array of gateways
(two or four, eight or twelve)
channel light outward-bound;
it frees a lucent flood
and allows a stasis.

Within the flat layers,
a sequence of chambers
(one or three, five or ten)
capture light inward-board;
It fuels a lucent well
and builds a kinesis.

The syrup column

In a great wax chamber,
a column of syrup
oozes from the ceiling,
perfectly thick and dense,
and seeping languidly
through a valve in the floor.

Ringing the column base
is a sugar halo
of crystallised white dust
to which flies congregate.
Any which brush the flow
are swallowed through the valve.

A body, in error,
slips on the sugar dust,
is snared by the column
and struggles to squirm free.
Syrup smothers their cries
and soon they suffocate.

Stuck fast in the valve beak,
they impede the outflow.
The syrup spills over
in rude folds on the floor,
rippling to the ceiling,
sealing the chamber tight.

The pressure apexes,
breaking up the body,
tearing it through the valve,
letting the syrup drain
from slick and glossy walls
the chamber then empty.

Dead flies slide down the valve,
smudging the wet halo.
The air is sweet and rich,
the wax dark and golden.
Until new flies return,
the chamber is silent.

IN EXCESS
OF FREEDOM

The version of No Freedom Too Total which was a finalist in the Proverse Prize 2023 included the foregoing poems but not the following three poems, which were written only subsequently, and unlike the foregoing poems, were written in Perth and not Hong Kong.

The wave, the soul, the spirit

There is a rippling wave
which has felt an impact:
an error in fixed time;
a wound of the future
whose damage self-upsets;
movement which never stills.

There is a stilling wave
which has felt an impact:
an event in lost time;
an act of the human
that nature reconciles;
stasis that never breaks.

On the crest of the wave,
a spirit strikes a soul:
the phallus tightening;
the anus widening;
cum flowing through hard pipes;
blood pouring from soft chutes.

In the wake of the wave,
a soul strikes a spirit:
two hands find pairs of holes;
two lungs squeezed into cores;
bright sensations lapsing;
complex patterns ending.

The soul made manifest:
breached by the human hand,
an act of effluxion
which stands for completion;
a splitting into parts
in which the whole is found.

The spirit made perfect:
snuffed by the human will,
an act of destruction
which stands for completion;
a massing of a whole
from which no parts are split.

The sower and the reaper

A sower, in the field,
makes talk with the reaper:
"How ruthless is the sun?
It seems there are two things:
the spirit that endures,,
and the spirit that breaks.

I have tribulations
so painful I can't breathe:
blood on my fingertips,
blisters across my skin;
some fields grow, others don't;
how it is make no sense.

I could have been elsewhere
but I brought myself here:
there are choices I made;
there are paths I skirted;
but one thing is certain:
we all reap what we sow."

A reaper, in the field,
makes talk with the sower:
"How callous is the frost?
It seems there are two things:
the labour that succeeds,
And the labour that fails.

I have disappointments
so many I can't count:
blight in the intestines,
decay throughout my mouth;
some fields live, others don't;
why it is means nothing.

I should have known better
but I brought myself here:
there are truths I can't face;
there are walls I can't scale;
but one thing is certain:
we all reap what we sow."

I see the face of God

I look from left to right
and see a human form:
a foot, a heart, a hand;
is it my companion?
As they appear to me,
I see the face of God.

I reach out to touch them
and my hands just touch soil,
but as the ages pass,
their form remains intact.
Of their human image
I am a reflection.

By a change of their heart
they could destroy my life;
make me cry endless tears
and endure untold pain.
Though I might never heal,
I will love them the same.

I look from right to left,
and see a Godlike form:
a spine, a valve, a hand;
is it my protector?
As they appear to me,
I see the face of God.

I reach out to touch them
but their surface splinters,
and though the ages pass,
in time they re-emerge.
Of their perfect image
I am an abstraction.

By the force of their will
they could destroy my life;
take me far from my home
and cast me towards death.
But even once I die,
I will love them the same.

AFTERWORD

As noted in the foreword, each of the poems in this collection has six stanzas. Each stanza has six lines. Each line has six syllables.

The form aims to use correct grammar, not break words over more than one line, and use language that is as natural as possible and which can be read aloud.

Poems in this form can be called '666 poems'. They have also been described as 'hexagrammatical poems' or 'two-dimensional verbal cubes'.

Six is the most harmonious number. It divides cleanly by numbers one, two and three. It multiplies into other harmonious numbers, such as twelve, eighteen, twenty-four and thirty-six. On the face of a clock, the numbers in the cardinal positions are three, six, nine and twelve.

Poems in this form have internal patterns, harmonies, accords and 'echoes'. Some of the poems consist of two interlocking halves; some of the poems consist of three interlocking thirds; some consist of six interlocking sixths. Certain motifs recur at regular points within a single poem, and within a series of poems. These patterns can be considered a kind of 'deep rhyme'.

A patterned poem, like a patterned object, can be considered a thing of beauty or an *objet d'art*. It is a multi-paneled structure, like a crystal, a prism, a hall of mirrors or a cage.

Like a puzzle, the writing of a poem is a game the poet plays with themselves, and the reading of a poem is a game the reader plays with themselves.

Poems in this form can assist in achieving a state of concentration, relaxation, meditation, hallucination, trance or hypnosis.

PRIOR PUBLICATION ACKNOWLEDGEMENTS

Two men walking was previously published in *Creatrix* (the journal of WA Poets Inc) as *A man walks* in Issue 53, June 2021.

Two people, two vessels was previously published as a commissioned work as part of the Polytechnic University of Hong Kong Fashion MFA Graduate Show in August 2021.

The shielder, the shielded' was previously published in *Mingled Voices 6* (an anthology publication of Proverse Hong Kong) in April 2022.

China Banks of Freedom and Control and *China Banks of Desire and Hatred* were previously published in Apocalypse Confidential as *The China Bank of Freedom in dialogue with the China Bank of Control; The China Bank of Desire in dialogue with the China Bank of Hatred* in August 2022.

11th hour was previously published as a commissioned work as part of *RECESS*, an exhibition by artists Jay Staples and Stephen Brameld which showed at 1b Pakenham Street, Fremantle, Western Australia in October 2022.

Beatrice outlines the ascent was previously published in the Journal of the Australian-Irish Heritage Association in 2022.

The first dream: The brothels of Jinan and Taiyuan, The second dream: The dungeons of Chengdu and Chongqing and *The third dream: The escorts of Ningbo and Wenzhou* were previously published in Apocalypse Confidential as, respectively, *The dreams of Jinan and Taiyuan, The dreams of Chengdu and Chongqing* and *The dreams of Ningbo and Wenzhou* in April 2023.

Ferdiad and Cú Chulainn meet for battle was previously published in *Creatrix* (the journal of WA Poets Inc) in Issue 64, March 2024.

I see the face of God was previously exhibited alongside an artwork of the same name by artists Jay Staples and Stephen Brameld, exhibited from 25 May to 15 June 2024 at the Holmes à Court Gallery in West Perth.

www.ingramcontent.com/pod-product-compliance
Lightning Source LLC
Chambersburg PA
CBHW071557040426
42452CB00008B/1210